People of the Bible

The Bible through stories and pictures

Moses of the Bulrushes

Moses of the Bulrushes

Retold by Catherine Storr
Pictures by Jim Russell

Methuen Children's Books
in association with Belitha Press Ltd

Pharaoh, the King of Egypt was worried.
He thought that there were already
too many Israelites living in Egypt,
and he saw that every year
there were more of them.
He thought they might join his enemies
to fight against him.
So he ordered the Israelite midwives
to kill all the boy babies
that were born to their women.

The midwives thought this was cruel
and against the wish of God.
They saved the babies,
and made excuses, saying,
'These Israelite women
have their babies so quickly,
we can't get there in time to kill any of them.'

One Israelite mother hid her baby boy
for three months after he was born.
Then she knew she couldn't hide him any longer.
She made a cradle of bulrushes and mud,
and put the baby in it.
Then she floated the cradle
among the reeds of the river.
She told her daughter Miriam
to hide near the river
to see what would happen.

Presently Pharaoh's daughter, the Princess,
came down to the river to wash herself.
She found the cradle of bulrushes in the reeds,
and picked up the baby.

Then Moses' sister came out of hiding.
'Do you want a nurse for this baby?' she asked.
When the Princess said she did,
the girl fetched her own mother.
The Princess said to the woman,
'Take this child and nurse it for me.'

The boy was called Moses, which means
'One found in the water.'
He grew up in Egypt,
knowing that he was really an Israelite,
although the Egyptian Princess had found him.

One day he saw an Egyptian hitting an Israelite.
Moses looked this way and that way,
and when he saw that there was no one else there,
he killed the Egyptian.

But the next day he found two Israelites fighting.
When he asked them why, one of them said,
'Don't tell us to stop! You killed an Egyptian.'
Moses knew that if Pharaoh heard of this,
he would punish him. He was frightened,
so he left Egypt and went to live
in the land of Midian.
He pretended to be an Egyptian
because it would be safer.

When he was there, he rested by a well.
He saw the shepherds of the place
driving away some girls,
who wanted to draw water
for their father's sheep and goats.
Moses stood up to the shepherds.
He helped the girls to draw water
for their flock.

When the girls came back early from the fields,
their father, who was a priest, was surprised.
They told him that an Egyptian
had helped them water the flock.
So Jethro, their father, called Moses
into his tent to eat.
Later he gave Moses his daughter, Zipporah,
to be his wife.

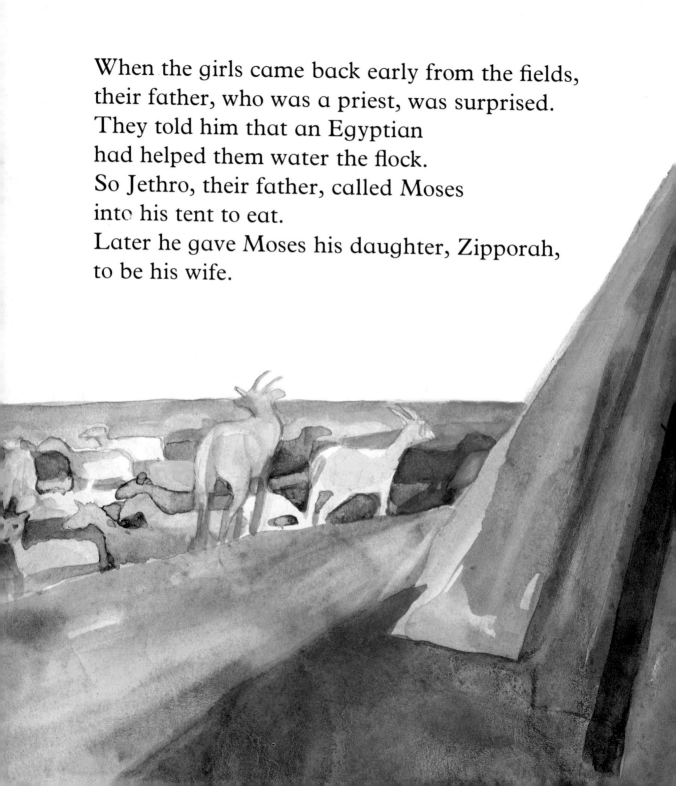

One day, when Moses was out
with his flock of sheep and goats,
he saw a bush in flames.
But although the bush was on fire,
it did not burn up.
Moses went closer to see what was happening,
and he heard God speak to him
out of the burning bush.

God said to Moses, 'Take off your shoes,
for this is holy ground.
I am the God of your fathers,
of Abraham, of Isaac and of Jacob.'
Then Moses hid his face,
for he was afraid to look at God.

God said, 'I know that my people,
the children of Israel,
suffer great hardships in Egypt.
I am going to deliver them,
and bring them out of Egypt.'

God said, 'I will bring them to a good land,
a large land, a land flowing with milk and honey.'
Moses said, 'Why should Pharaoh take any notice
of me, if I tell him this?
And what shall I say to the children of Israel?'
God said,
'Tell them that I am the God of their fathers.
Say that I AM THAT I AM.'

Moses said, 'Suppose they don't believe me?'
God said, 'What is that in your hand?'
Moses said, 'It is a rod.'
God said, 'Throw it on the ground.'
Moses did and the rod was changed into a serpent.
Moses ran away.
God said, 'Put out your hand
and pick up the serpent by the tail.'
Then the serpent changed back into a rod.

Moses was still uncertain of what he could do.
He said, 'I can't talk well or quickly.
No one will listen to me.'
But God said, 'I will help you to speak.
You have a brother, Aaron,
who is very good at talking.
I shall help both of you.'

So Moses and Aaron went down into Egypt.

They told the children of Israel
that they had been sent by God
to lead them out of their captivity in Egypt.
They should journey to another country, they said,
a land flowing with milk and honey,
which would be safe and fertile.
But Moses knew it would be a hard task
to persuade Pharaoh to let the people go.

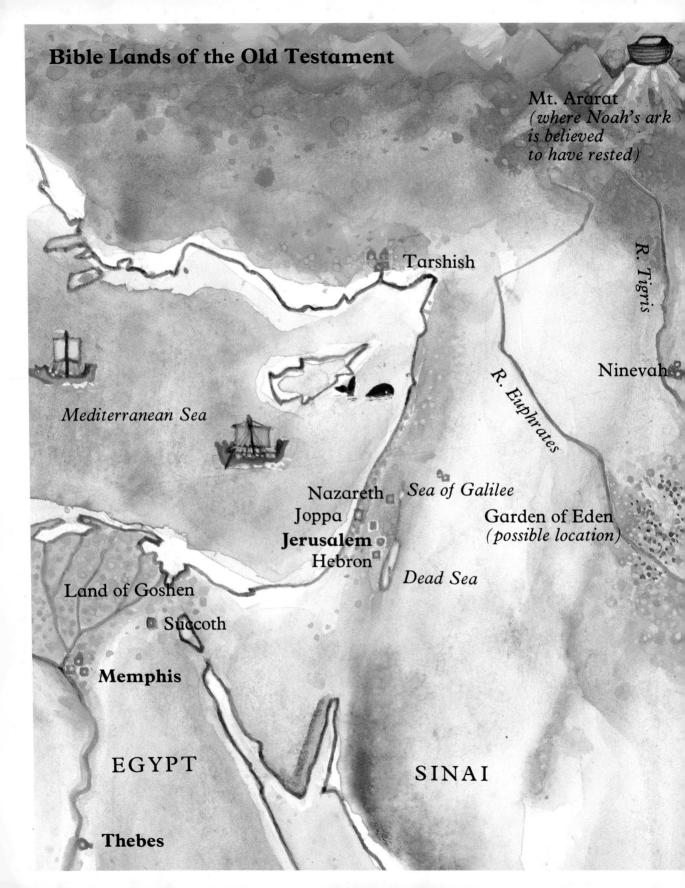

Bible Lands of the Old Testament

Mt. Ararat
*(where Noah's ark
is believed
to have rested)*

Tarshish

R. Tigris

Ninevah

R. Euphrates

Mediterranean Sea

Nazareth

Sea of Galilee

Joppa

Jerusalem

Garden of Eden
(possible location)

Hebron

Dead Sea

Land of Goshen

Succoth

Memphis

EGYPT

SINAI

Thebes